Original title:
Wristbands of Tomorrow

Copyright © 2025 Creative Arts Management OÜ
All rights reserved.

Author: Nora Sinclair
ISBN HARDBACK: 978-1-80586-167-6
ISBN PAPERBACK: 978-1-80586-639-8

Interwoven with Tomorrow's Aspirations

In a world where dreams are worn,
Fashioned from bright threads, all adorned.
Colors twist like a wild dance,
Promises stitched in a joyful prance.

Here's a band for your wildest hopes,
Woven tight with fabric ropes.
Wear it snug, don't let it slip,
Or it might start doing the moonwalk trip!

It whispers tales of future quests,
A little charm that never rests.
With every flick, a grin appears,
As it plots your fun through laughter and cheers.

So grab your flair, make a bold choice,
Let them chatter, let them rejoice!
For each twist and every loop,
Brings laughter to this vibrant troupe.

Traces of Hearts in Every Stitch

A little thread, a laugh so bright,
They hold our secrets, clutch them tight.
With every tug, they stretch and sway,
In silly colors, they dance and play.

They promise joy and a goofy grin,
As we forget the mess we're in.
Fashion faux pas become our pride,
With tangled love we cannot hide.

Harmonies Bound in Crafted Bands

A funky twist of fabric bold,
We wear our stories, laugh untold.
In colors loud, they sing the tune,
Matching chaos like a cartoon.

A band of friends, a cheerful bunch,
Our outfits clash, but who needs a hunch?
With every stitch, a giggle's stitched,
In mischief's name, we are bewitched.

Dreams Embroidered in Time's Embrace

In dreams we weave, with threads of cheer,
As tangled dreams bring laughter near.
With every twist, a silly plot,
They capture memories we forgot.

From morning mishaps to midnight chats,
These goofy charms wear our spats.
A sprinkle of chaos, a dash of fun,
Our handcrafted tales have just begun.

Tapestry of Unseen Connections

When threads collide in vibrant glee,
Our silly smiles are the best decree.
Crafted knots that wiggle and flop,
We'll never stop, we'll never drop.

In every loop, a silly jest,
A cozy vibe when we're at our best.
Jumbling colors, a comical sight,
Tangled friendships, our hearts take flight.

Hopes Encased in Colorful Ties

In hues so bright, they dance and sway,
Each twist a wish for a brighter day.
Like rubber bands stretched to their max,
They hold our dreams, no need for hacks.

In laughter's grip, we tie them tight,
A fashion statement, a playful sight.
They jingle-jangle as we prance,
Casting spells in this silly dance.

Links to the World Ahead

With colors that pop and giggles galore,
Each link a story, always wanting more.
They're quirky treasures worn with pride,
Unlocking joy, we wear them side by side.

From the office to the park we roam,
These loops of laughter feel just like home.
They jostle with glee upon our wrists,
A rainbow round-up that can't be missed.

Threads that Bind Generations

From grandmas' tales to babies' grins,
These threads of humor do all the spins.
Wrapped around wrists, they tie us tight,
Each knot a memory, pure delight.

With secrets shared from old to new,
They giggle in colors of bright pink and blue.
A family circus, a joyful knot,
Binding us up in a lovely lot.

Chronicles Woven with Progress

Here we weave tales in patterns bold,
Of future laughs that never get old.
Each thread a giggle, a punchline fun,
We'll laugh together till the day is done.

In kooky styles, the stories sprout,
Dancing through time with a playful shout.
These woven tales take us afar,
A tapestry bright, our quirky bazaar.

Dreams Threaded Through Time

Tiny threads that weave and spin,
They promise joy, never a grin.
A world where fashion gets quite bold,
With every color, stories told.

Dancing like a squishy bread,
Around the wrist, thoughts are fed.
Laughter springs from silly sights,
As dreams take off on magical flights.

Gestures of the Future in Color

Fingers pointing to the sky,
Would you like some jelly pie?
In shades of blue and vibrant green,
They make us laugh, they make us keen.

With every twist and every turn,
The future's bright, just wait your turn.
Colorful gags at every seam,
As smiles pop like an ice cream dream.

Woven Wishes of the Mind's Eye

In the realm where thoughts fluff up,
A wish gets woven with a hiccup.
Imaginations dance and sing,
While broccoli becomes a crown to bring.

Tangled threads of what is mine,
Beads of laughter, bright and fine.
Each twist a moment left behind,
In future's hands, what will we find?

Fragments of the Yet-to-Come

Pieces scattered, bits of fun,
Hopes that twinkle like the sun.
As we piece together these squares,
Giggles echo through fresh air.

Cut and paste our silly ways,
In shades that shift, like sunny days.
Fragments here and fragments there,
Make a future beyond compare.

Chronicles of Change Threaded in Fabric

In a bustling town where colors gleam,
Fabrics talk louder than you'd ever dream.
They whisper stories of days gone by,
And stretch with laughter, oh me, oh my.

Worn by rebels, and the wise old man,
Flaunting patterns like a rainbow plan.
Each stitch a giggle, each seam a cheer,
Let's dance in threads that don't disappear.

Hues of Hope Along Life's Pathway.

In the market square with a vibrant flare,
Hues of crazy colors dance in the air.
A purple cape for the baker's cat,
With neon shoes, let's make a splat!

Life's a canvas, let's paint it bright,
With polka dots and stripes, what a sight!
A plaid umbrella on a sunny day,
Who knew fabric could make us sway?

Bindings of the Future

Tangled threads in a brilliant array,
Bindings of fate are here to play.
A slipknot in laughter, a bow in grace,
In the fabric of life, we find our place.

Socks that don't match but wear a smile,
A rainbow of choices, let's stay awhile.
In knots of joy, we spin and twirl,
Tomorrow's fabric is a world to unfurl.

Threads of Anticipation

With anticipation, we tie up our dreams,
In threads of laughter, impossibly seams.
A quirky stitch that knows no bounds,
In the tapestry of life, joy resounds.

Woven together with a wink and a grin,
Who knew a thread could let happiness in?
Tripping on laughter with every loop,
Join the fabric party, let's all regroup!

Keepsakes of Tomorrow's Dreamers

Beneath the stars, they twiddle their thumbs,
Dreaming of futures with popcorn and drums.
Sticky notes on their foreheads they wear,
Ideas so wild, you wonder, who dare?

Giggles abound, as they spark a new craze,
Designing bright snacks, that could really amaze.
With marshmallow rainbows and donuts that sing,
Tomorrow's dreamers make everything bling!

Reflections Created by Fabric

In fabric they see, a world full of glee,
Trousers that dance, and shirts that agree.
With patches of smiles stitched in with care,
They strut with a flair, causing neighbors to stare.

A cape made of socks that smells like delight,
Turning laundry-day blues into pure comic light.
Their wardrobes are wizardry, crazy but neat,
Each outfit a riddle, each twist a sweet treat!

Tapestries of Tomorrow Unfurled

From threads of the future, they weave and they snip,
Creating a dance floor that's ready to flip.
With patterns that bounce, and colors that sing,
They fashion the night like it's a grand fling.

Juggling their mishaps, their humor's a blast,
Every laugh echoing, no moment too fast.
A tapestry woven with giggles and cheers,
Crafting the sunset of whimsical years.

Strands of Time Intertwined

As ages collide, with a chuckle and grin,
Past, present and future, let the fun begin!
Frogs in tuxedos and hats made of cheese,
Time loops like licorice, bendy with ease.

In this merry mix, they fashion a bind,
Where moments are jellybeans space designed.
With laughter like glue, they stick together tight,
Crafting new memories to brighten the night!

Bracelets of Unseen Potential

A loop of colors on my wrist,
They promise things I can't resist.
From funky charms to shiny beads,
They hold my hopes and silly needs.

A stretch of fabric, a twist of fate,
They giggle at me, 'Wait, don't be late!'
Each knot a secret, each clasp a dream,
In a world where nothing's what it seems.

Ties that Bind Time's Journey

These ties hold moments, short and sweet,
Like candy wrappers beneath my feet.
A tug of laughter, a spin of glee,
Binding fun times, just you and me.

They tickle time with every tug,
A twist, a turn, a wacky mug.
With every day they stretch and strain,
But through it all, they still remain.

Patterns of Change Yet Unfolded

My arm's a canvas, colors bold,
Each pattern tells a story untold.
Like socks that dance in mismatched pairs,
They whisper jokes as style declares.

With polka dots and zigzag stripes,
They dream of high-flyin' delights.
They laugh at trends that come and go,
Their quirky vibes are in full flow.

Adornments of New Beginnings

These trinkets shine like stars at dawn,
Each trinket's tale is never worn.
They flip the script on life's old page,
Frolicking free, refusing cage.

With every twist, they promise cheer,
In a world that often disappears.
A laugh, a cheer, a wild spin,
As we embrace our jolly grin.

Bands of Unseen Horizons

In a world of fabric bright,
We sport our colors, what a sight!
Twisting knots and loops galore,
Adventures wait behind each door.

Stretching, pulling, they don't break,
A stretchy promise, for goodness' sake.
They hold our dreams, our hopes, our plans,
Though they might look like salad bands!

Ties that Connect Us All

These little loops, they're quite the deal,
They bond us all, that's the appeal.
From tiny tots to the old and wise,
Each one holds a surprise like fries!

Look at my wrist, it's quite the game,
With colors flashing, tight like fame.
The one with dots is really neat,
But the rainbow's just so hard to beat!

Emblems of Evolving Dreams

Strapping dreams on every wrist,
With hopes and wishes, we can't resist.
They change and shift like morning dew,
But never fear, they stick like glue!

A unicorn here, a pizza slice there,
From lava lamps to teddy bears.
Each gives a wink, a nudge, a cheer,
Promising laughs from ear to ear!

Straps of Hope and Change

Each strap we wear is quite a tale,
From bad jokes shared to pizza fail.
They stretch and mold and twist just right,
A bobbing dance, pure delight!

Hope is woven in every thread,
Who knew such fun could come from red?
Colors and patterns, laughter too,
Each one whispers, 'Just be you!'

Chronicles in Each Woven Strand

In colors bold and bright,
We share our silly tales,
Each strand a joyful link,
As laughter never fails.

With every twist and turn,
A memory we weave,
From pranks to crazy times,
In all we dare believe.

Strands of neon laughter,
And jokes that never fade,
Together we create,
A riotous cascade.

So here's to silly dreams,
In a tangled, fun parade,
With every thread unbound,
Our friendship's serenade.

Cords of Courage and Progress

Oh, look at this haphazard braid,
With mismatched colors, bold,
Like heroes of old passed down,
In tales that are retold.

A tangle of wild ambition,
With knots of goofy cheer,
Each twist a brave decision,
We wear without a fear.

With courage as our fabric,
We dance through thick and thin,
And laugh as we embrace,
The wackiest of wins.

So hold on tight, my pal,
This chaos feels just right,
In laughter, we find strength,
A whimsical delight.

Patterns Weaved in Shared Hope

In patterns bright and funny,
Our hopes are tightly sewn,
With every giggle shared,
A joyous undertone.

Each loop a little secret,
A bond that we create,
With humor stitched so snug,
In every twist of fate.

From mishaps to triumphs,
Our stories start to bloom,
In every single fiber,
There's laughter in the room.

United by the chaos,
We dance like silly fools,
Together we're a masterpiece,
In the fabric of our tools.

Tributes to What Lies Ahead

To futures filled with laughter,
And plans that make us grin,
We tie our dreams together,
And let the fun begin.

With every stretch of visions,
We leap, we laugh, we play,
In bonds that brightly shimmer,
As we dance through the day.

So here's a toast to mischief,
And lighthearted design,
With threads of joy and courage,
We boldly intertwine.

In the tapestry of friendship,
What lies ahead feels bright,
Together we will face it,
With humor as our light.

Weaving the Future's Design

In a loom of dreams we spin,
Colors bright and fibers thin.
Stitching laughter, thread by thread,
Making jokes as we are fed.

Fingers dance with crafty spree,
Creating patterns wild and free.
A tapestry of quirky styles,
Where every knot brings endless smiles.

From cotton candy, trends accrue,
Fashion statements fresh and new.
The fabric hides our secrets bold,
In swirls of tones, our tales are told.

Fabric of Unfolding Stories

In threads of whimsy, fun unfolds,
Each stitch a story yet untold.
We craft adventures with a grin,
A patchwork of where we have been.

With every loop, a giggle spins,
In the weaving game, everyone wins.
Twists and turns, both big and small,
Our fabric catches joy for all.

Promise Embedded in Every Thread

In every fiber, a pledge we weave,
Promising giggles, if you believe.
A sassy stitch, a playful knot,
A whimsical tale that can't be bought.

In vibrant hues our futures gleam,
A wacky world stitched from a dream.
With every twirl, the laughter spreads,
A funky saga, joy in our heads.

Connections Worn with Pride

Worn upon our wrists, a badge we sport,
In colors that dance, a newfound sort.
A rally of friends, so wildly paired,
With threads of laughter, we've all shared.

Banter bright like neon lights,
Together we scale the highest heights.
A symphony of giggles, loud and clear,
Woven together, we hold life dear.

Cuffs of the Coming Age

In a world where colors clash,
Bright bands jingle with a splash.
Worn on wrists, they tell a tale,
Of adventures big and small, without fail.

They glow like neon in the night,
Dancing with laughter, what a sight!
Some say they're magic, others feign,
But every one hides a silly strain.

With slogans bold, and jokes to share,
Wrapped around, a friendship rare.
Pull on a cuff to catch a laugh,
Join the party, here's your pass!

So let's embrace this vibrant craze,
With cuffs that brighten all our days.
A twist of fate, a wink, a cheer,
Fun's not far when laughter's here!

Fables Woven in Threads

Tales of old stuck in a weave,
Fashioned on wrists, they never leave.
A stretch of fabric, a twist or two,
Every thread whispers something new.

Once a dragon wore a band,
Supposedly crafted by a hand.
Now it's just a tale we tell,
Of fables woven - oh so well!

Strap one on, and take a chance,
You might just start a crazy dance.
Who knew a thread could make us grin,
And wrap our heads in joy within?

So here's to stories, fun, and flair,
With bands that love the wild air.
Wear your fable, share your dream,
Life's a laugh, or so it seems!

Symbols of Tomorrow's Promise

Symbols wrapped around each wrist,
Promises made, none are missed.
With every color, every style,
We trick the fates to make them smile.

Each morning brings a brand new quest,
Will it sparkle? Will it jest?
Laugh with fate, and dance away,
Tomorrow's bright, so let's not stray.

They're signs of hope with a twist of fun,
Their silent giggles weigh a ton.
A nudge, a wink, they're bold and brash,
These quirky pieces lead a clash!

So wear your symbols, let them shine,
In the chaos, we'll align.
No need to worry, just be free,
With laughter wrapped around like glee!

Armbands of Infinite Possibilities

Infinite dreams strapped on tight,
With armbands that giggle just right.
Take a leap, unleash the fun,
With every color, we can run!

They promise laughter, a dash of cheer,
In every corner, they are near.
Take your pick, the one that fits,
And see how joy endlessly flits.

A flick of the wrist, you can't resist,
Armbands that laugh, a twist of bliss.
Unseen powers in shades of glee,
They whisper secrets, can you see?

So buckle up, and join the ride,
With these bands, let dreams collide.
Tomorrow's woes might just dissolve,
In a playful world, we all evolve!

Interwoven Adventures Awaiting

In a place where threads collide,
We wear our dreams, an endless ride.
Colors swirl in a funky dance,
Mismatched patterns, a world of chance.

Beads and twirls, a silly sight,
A cat caught in a scarf's delight.
Fabrics argue, a tussle of fun,
While we giggle beneath the sun.

Beyond the Cloth

Stripes and spots, a patchwork tale,
As fables rise, we set our sail.
With every loop, a laugh is spun,
Life's a giggle, we've just begun.

Each twist holds a secret spark,
A story shared in the park.
Threads so bright, they tease the eye,
Making friends as we stroll by.

Futures Await

Glimmers of hope on our wrists we tie,
Crafted dreams that soar and fly.
Can't tell if it's style or jest,
A fashion statement, we're all so blessed.

Hitch a ride on a thread so bold,
Every color a mystery unfolds.
In this jumbled, vibrant show,
We dance together, letting go.

Symbols of Progress in Motion

From tangled yarns, we find our way,
Woven giggles brighten our day.
With every twist, a playful cheer,
Future's crafty, we have no fear.

A heaping laugh tucked in each stitch,
As we prank the world, just a little bit.
Patterns forming, a dance so fine,
Together we weave, our fates align.

The Art of Shaping What's Next

Crafty hands will shape our quest,
The silliest things become the best.
Knotted ideas bounce with glee,
In this fabric fun, we're wild and free.

Let's plot our course with mismatched flair,
Giggles echo through the air.
Every piece a jumbled thread,
In this laughter, we're utterly wed.

Stitching Moments

In a world of colors bright,
We stitch together pure delight.
With threads that dance and twirl,
We craft a happy, vibrant swirl.

A seam here, a patch so bold,
Our quirky stories start to unfold.
With needle, thread, and a playful grin,
Each tiny stitch, a place to begin.

Crafting Futures

With scissors sharp and smiles wide,
We cut through fabric, side by side.
Each snip a wish, each fold a dream,
Creating futures that brightly beam.

Stitching plans on a fabric scroll,
We pour our laughter into the whole.
With each fold, we shape the fun,
Gathering sunshine, one by one.

The Pulse of Endless Horizons

Our crafting table's a wonderland,
With glitter, tinsel, all at hand.
We weave our hopes with threads of cheer,
Each tiny pulse whispers, 'Adventure's near!'

Like a wristwatch that loves to sing,
We tick-tock tales of zany fling.
In every stitch, a giggle hides,
As futures unfold on colorful rides.

Celestial Strands of Hope

In a cosmos filled with quirky flair,
We tie the stars with utmost care.
Galactic threads of laughter spun,
Creating bracelets that weigh a ton!

Each twinkle tells a tale so bright,
Of cosmic giggles dancing at night.
We pull the moon down, feel its glow,
Crafting dreams from the magic we sow.

Fabricated Dreams for Days Ahead

We gather scraps and bits of fun,
As laughter threads get the job done.
Fabrics filled with joy and glee,
Creating futures as wild as can be!

Sewing smiles into every seam,
We're fabricating the ultimate dream.
With each snip, a new plan unfurls,
In our stitched world, adventure swirls.

Futures Bound in Fabric

In a realm where fabric flies,
Stitching dreams 'neath sunny skies.
With every thread, a story spins,
Where laughter reigns and joy begins.

Colors clash in playful schemes,
Tangled up in silly dreams.
Wobbly patterns dance and sway,
Tickling thoughts that drift away.

Patterns shouting, 'Look at me!'
Crafted with such playful glee.
Every twist and every turn,
In this fabric, laughter burns.

Sewing futures, one by one,
Crafting fun beneath the sun.
With a snip and playful wink,
Life's a stitch; don't overthink!

Threads of Tomorrow's Embrace

Threads of joy, they intertwine,
Warping futures, yours and mine.
Ticklish textures make us grin,
As each new layer finds its kin.

In a mix of polka dots,
Laughter bursts in playful knots.
Loopy loops and zigzag lines,
Where imagination brightly shines.

Gather round for fabric tales,
Whimsical winds fill up the sails.
Soft embraces, stitched to last,
In moments shared, we'll have a blast.

Sew along this happy path,
With a giggle and a laugh.
For in the threads that weave our fate,
Fun awaits, let's celebrate!

Colors Woven into Destiny

Colors merge in wild delight,
A canvas of chaos, what a sight!
Candy hues and floppy hats,
Bring on the giggles, zoom like bats.

Brushing past in vibrant hues,
Creativity the only muse.
Dancing shades in bright display,
Painting joy in every way.

A patchwork quilt of mishaps bright,
Silly moments, pure delight.
Spin the wheel, let colors flow,
In playful patterns, let's all glow.

In the mix, we laugh and cheer,
Every stitch, a friend is near.
This tapestry of joy unfolds,
With every thread, a tale retold!

Echoes of Tomorrow's Promise

Echoes giggle through the air,
Promising fun beyond compare.
Sassy prints and funky styles,
Bringing forth those joyful smiles.

Bouncing colors, dance away,
Like a carousel, they sway.
Little whispers, "Join the fun,"
Under the sparkly, shining sun.

Crafted dreams in every seam,
Life's a product of the beam.
Jumbo buttons, quirky things,
Harvesting joy that laughter brings.

With every tug, we spin and groove,
Finding our own silly move.
In the echoes of what will be,
Let's stitch together, you and me!

Bonds Beyond the Now

A thread of laughter, bright and spry,
Links of joy that flitter high.
Wrapped around like a playful tune,
Future whispers beneath the moon.

Connections made from giggles and tales,
Stitched together with silly trails.
Hold on tight, don't let it slip,
Time's a ride, it's quite the trip!

Colors clash like socks on the line,
Every hue tells a story divine.
In every twist, a memory bends,
Laughter echoes, as humor blends.

Narrative Threads of What's to Come

In the loom of time, we weave and play,
Silly patterns brighten the gray.
Every loop carries a cheer,
Tomorrow's tales are spinning near.

Jumbled thoughts on a cotton thread,
Each moment tickles, never dread.
Dancing lines that never tire,
A waltz at dawn, oh what a fire!

Past and future are equal parts,
Drawing smiles in all our hearts.
Grab your friend, let's make a scene,
Crafting dreams in shades of green.

Intersection of Time and Fabric

Time winks with a stitch and a knot,
Closing gaps and giving it a shot.
Threads of laughter cross and tie,
In this patchwork, we learn to fly.

Every misstep, a dance we embrace,
Hooks of humor find their place.
Fabrics dash like squirrels on the run,
Time's fabric is woven with fun!

Patterns collide in a cheerful spree,
What's next? Oh, who could foresee?
Let's tie the past to a rubber band,
Bouncing forward, hand in hand.

Markers of Unwritten Journeys

Invisible maps mark each step we take,
Puns and giggles, that's how we make.
Milestones built from quips and drapes,
In the garden of fate, our laughter shapes.

In every tick, a joke is found,
Whirling moments, all around.
Each path twists like spaghetti plates,
Life's a feast, let's open the gates!

With every story, a giggle's cast,
Time's jokester makes moments last.
So grab your compass, and don't forget,
Fun awaits, you bet your pet!

Embraces of Time Yet to Come

In a world where colors dance,
Futures wrapped in silly chance.
Watch as fortune twists and bends,
With every tick, the laughter blends.

Straps of joy upon our skin,
Every second's cheeky grin.
Time's embrace is quite a treat,
Wiggling arms make life's beat sweet.

So gather round, and clasp them tight,
Adventures call beneath the light.
With giggles loud and smiles wide,
We'll flip the clock and take a ride.

As minutes laugh and seconds play,
These quirky bands will lead the way.
Together we'll make memories soar,
With every twist, we'll ask for more!

Links to Tomorrow's Journey

Straps that connect our whims and dreams,
Tangled up in goofy schemes.
Adventure waits with every pull,
Embracing life, our hearts are full.

With each clasp, a story flips,
Hand in hand, we take wild trips.
Traveling paths of laughs and cheer,
Where silly thoughts draw us near.

Links that jingle with delight,
Brightening every awkward sight.
Every step a dance absurd,
In this journey, joy's the word.

What's ahead? We just can't say,
But with these links, we'll find our way.
Embrace the mess, the quirky fun,
Tomorrow's magic has begun!

The Fabric of Dreams Unfolding

Threads that weave with laughter loud,
Stitching futures, quite unbowed.
With every twirl, a whim is born,
In this fabric, silliness worn.

Patterns clash, colors collide,
Through tangled paths, we'll take a ride.
Every loop a jest or tale,
In this fabric, we cannot fail.

Snippets of joy in every seam,
Crafting moments, living the dream.
We'll wear our quirks both bold and bright,
Together weaving through the night.

So grab a thread and let's create,
A tapestry of laughs, first-rate.
With memories sewn and silly spun,
In this fabric, we are one!

Adornments of the New Dawn

Shiny baubles, oh what glee,
Hanging brightly, just wait and see.
As the sun peeks through the haze,
These adornments bring us praise.

With every trinket comes a smile,
Fun and laughter, a joyful style.
Glistening rays, we jump and sway,
Starting new and silly each day.

Jangled gems that sparkle bright,
Chasing shadows, bringing light.
With giggles shared and hearts so free,
These shiny charms, just you and me.

Dawn's embrace is wild and neat,
Every moment feels so sweet.
Adorned with joy, we'll laugh and run,
In this new day, let's have some fun!

Ribbons of Fashioned Aspirations

Tied around a hopeful wrist,
A dream that thinks it can persist,
Colorful threads in a flashy spree,
Each twist whispers, "Look at me!"

Sunny shades of pink and blue,
Stuck in fashion's endless queue,
They promise luck with a playful wink,
But snag on chairs when you don't think!

Sneaky squirrels might take a glance,
And ask if they can join the dance,
With curious eyes and twitchy tails,
They ponder how your wrist unveils!

So tie them tight—avoid the throng,
For every band can feel so strong,
Wear them proud, or let them fray,
Just make sure they don't flee away!

Symbols Carved in Time's Embrace

Clocks with hands that dance and twirl,
Fashioned symbols give a whirl,
Each tick tock makes a silly sound,
It's where chaos and fun are found!

Rubber bands that stretch and twist,
Hold the chaos with a fist,
They laugh and stretch beyond their bounds,
Just don't get snagged on playground grounds!

Doodles etched on every hue,
Tell tales of mishaps, make-do,
Like when they caught your sleeve just right,
And sent you soaring into flight!

Time's embrace, a funny jest,
Wrist wonders that never rest,
Each band sings a quirky tune,
Fashioned dreams beneath the moon!

Cuffs That Echo Dreams

Bright cuffs made of wishful threads,
Each one a tale, where laughter spreads,
Swirling hopes tied in a bow,
You might trip, but steal the show!

Echoes of laughter fill the air,
As one slips off without a care,
Then they bounce, make quite a scene,
Leaving you in awkward green!

Imagined worlds held on with glee,
You'd think they might set you free,
But follow you with silly prance,
Inviting everyone to dance!

Cuffs that chime with every wave,
Keep the silliness we crave,
In colorful tones that seem to giggle,
Wear them proudly, give a wiggle!

Adornments That Inspire Tomorrow

Bright baubles that shine and spin,
Worn by dreams that laugh and grin,
They spark ideas like fireflies,
Adorning hopes beneath the skies!

Each charm's a giggle, a whispered joke,
A playful wink, a teasing poke,
What do you think, do they have flair?
Just watch them dance without a care!

Bouncing thoughts like rubber balls,
They echo through the busy halls,
"Tomorrow's here!" they scream in fun,
As they twirlingly bask in sun!

With every twist, new dreams will sprout,
Beneath a sky of joyful shout,
So dwell in laughter, wear a smile,
These adornments last a while!

Vibrant Threads of Destiny

In a shop of colors bright,
I found a thread that danced with light.
It giggled as I wrapped it tight,
Claiming magic in every sight.

A neon green that winked at me,
A pink that sang, 'Just let it be!'
These threads connect in quirky spree,
Fashion's jest, how wild can we be?

With every twist, the laughter grows,
A style that nobody really knows.
My wrist now hosts a rainbow of pose,
Like a circus where humor flows.

Tomorrow's threads—so silly and grand,
Each a story, each a brand.
A tapestry sewn by hand,
In a world of fun, let's all stand.

Connections Beyond Tomorrow

In this realm of spunky threads,
Wit and whimsy dance like heads.
They tug and pull like playful kids,
A friendship formed, oh how it spreads!

These colorful bands from far-off lands,
Joke and jive on cartoon hands.
They whisper secrets, make their plans,
Woven laughter—no need for scans!

Each knot a giggle, each loop a jest,
A fashion show for the wild at best.
A rainbow of nonsense in a simple quest,
Who knew the future could be so blessed?

Tomorrow smiles in fiber and fun,
Twisting paths where we all run.
Join the parade, don't be outdone,
With threads so vibrant, we've just begun.

The Pulse of Future Fashions

In the future, trends go wild,
With a pulse that bounces like a child.
Wristy wonders, hilariously styled,
Fashion's a game, we're all reviled!

Check out this strap with cosmic flair,
It jokes and jives, without a care.
Spin it thrice—what's hiding there?
A world of giggles, beyond compare!

Each band a story, quirky yet true,
Colors clashing, a vibrant brew.
Silly shapes in every hue,
Fashion's pulse, let's all construe!

Let laughter lead in every stitch,
Wristy delights make humor rich.
We'll strut and dance, no need to switch,
Tomorrow's pulse—oh, what a glitch!

Echoes in Every Strand

Echoes of laughter in every thread,
A world where seriousness fled.
These quirky strands, joyfully spread,
Fashion's playground, where dreams are fed.

Each loop is a joke, each knot a pun,
Stringing together, oh what fun!
Threads tickling wrists, under the sun,
A merry parade—come join the run!

Colors clash like comic strips,
Wristy whispers from cosmic trips.
With every twist, the humor slips,
In delightful patterns, the laughter drips.

So here's to tomorrow, fun and bright,
Wear your joy as a badge of light.
Let's dance and jest, hold on tight,
In the echoes of threads, we find delight!

Luminaries in Colors Unseen

A rainbow wraps 'round my wrist,
Each hue a silly little twist,
Blue for the days I can't find my keys,
And green for the moments I sneeze.

Red for the lunch that I've misplaced,
And yellow for when I trip in haste,
Each color a giggle, a wink of fun,
In this circus of life, we all stand as one.

Purple's for mischief, stories to tell,
Like the time that I hiccuped and fell off a bell,
The orange shines bright like my morning toast,
It laughs at my troubles and plays like a ghost.

So here's to the colors that dance on my skin,
A painted adventure where chaos begins,
With every twist, I smile and I beam,
In this wild little world, we create our dream.

Fates Entwined in Physical Form

Two lives merged, a colorful thread,
A spark of laughter sets the tone instead,
When I duck, you duck, like a synchronized dance,
Our clumsy ballet ignites every chance.

With quirks that collide like bumper cars,
We race down life, finding joy among scars,
You bring out the mischief, I bring the cheer,
Together we conquer, with no hint of fear.

Side by side, we bread loaves of delight,
A flourish of shenanigans wrapped up tight,
Your misstep might trip me into a laugh,
But it's you by my side that keeps my path half.

In this tangled web of giggle and fate,
Our lives entwined, this journey is great,
For we're a pair, in this merry cocoon,
Masters of mayhem, we dance to our tune.

Bands of Resilience and Legacy

A band around my wrist, what a curious thing,
It bounces and jives, like a boisterous spring,
A badge of honor for moments I flub,
Or simply for days where I snugly rub.

Each twist tells a story, every curl has a laugh,
From karaoke crooning to wobbly giraffe,
These bands are my trophies, they hold up the fun,
Each giggle a memory, our lives all spun.

When fluff and whimsy collide with the real,
These bands bring to mind just how we feel,
"We fell off the stage?" a resounding cheer,
With laughter like lightning, we conquer our fear.

A swirl of resilience, they stay by my side,
Through puddles of giggles and slippery slides,
Each band a reminder, a joyful encore,
In this circus of life, we couldn't ask for more.

Bridges Worn Upon the Skin

A bridge of colors across my hand,
Stretches like dreams in a playful band,
Each slip and each slide a tiny connection,
A laughter-filled journey, a joyful direction.

As I raise my hand, the colors collide,
Creating a canopy, our giggles inside,
You slip on the yellow, I bounce in the green,
Together we craft silly moments unseen.

With every flick, a joke starts to fly,
The purple's a wink, while the orange says hi,
Bridges of laughter, they hold us secure,
In this knot of chaos, we always endure.

So wear your bright colors, let laughter entwine,
As we navigate life, a whimsical line,
For every bridge worn upon our skin,
Leads us to the giggles that always begin.

Emblems of a New Dawn

On my wrist, a twist of fate,
A colorful loop, now isn't that great!
It glimmers in the morning light,
An accessory that feels just right.

Like tiny rainbows on my arm,
They promise fun, they bring me charm.
They squeak and bounce, they dance and jive,
In this silly land, I feel alive!

Each one tells tales, oh what a game,
From bake sales to the silly name.
They'd play some tricks or rattle my bones,
Through laughter and joy, they're never alone.

So here I flaunt my silly style,
With vibrant bands, I'll walk the mile.
Making giggles where I roam,
In a quirky world, they are my home.

Luminescent Adornments of Dreams

Glowing bands dance in delight,
Like fireflies caught in the night's flight.
They flash and shimmer, oh what a show,
I chuckle softly, watch them glow.

Caught in the light, they'll have their say,
They whisper jokes in a bright ballet.
With colors swirling, my wrist's a stage,
Who knew style could be this outrageous?

Like playful puppies, they bark and play,
On my arm, they just won't stay.
A lighthearted army, all in a line,
Marching through life, oh how divine!

So join the fun, wear your own flair,
Let your spirit leap in the air.
With giggles and grins, we spread the cheer,
In our whimsical world, joy is here.

Tangles of Future's Fabric

My wrist is tangled, a colorful mess,
Like spaghetti strands, I must confess.
Each twist and turn, a story to tell,
In this merry chaos, I dwell.

A rainbow bungle, a vibrant thread,
They laugh at me, must be all in my head.
Sometimes they tangle, a rat's delight,
But who could be mad when it's this bright?

They jump and wiggle, a quirky crew,
In my cheerful chaos, they rarely feel blue.
With every twist, a giggle escapes,
I'll spin and twirl in these silly shapes!

Oh, my tangled friends, so full of cheer,
With every heartbeat, they draw near.
In a world so funny, let's all embrace,
These jumbled delights, our joyful space.

Mantles of Tomorrow's Whisper

On my wrist, a whimsic swirl,
Each layer of joy begins to unfurl.
They whisper secrets, soft and sweet,
These playful bands tap dance on my feet.

Each color tells stories, old and new,
They scheme and plot, what will they do?
With sudden wiggles, they make me grin,
In this hoopla, we all fit in!

They sometimes tangle, a comedy show,
But woven together, we steal the glow.
Jokes and laughter in every strand,
An ensemble of fun, all hand in hand.

So let's be silly and dance away,
With bright adornments to save the day.
In a world of nonsense, we'll give a cheer,
For every wrist, let's hold our dear!

Laces Tied with Aspirations

Laces weaving tales of dreams,
Tangled here, or so it seems.
Chasing hopes with every twist,
Watch them dance, you can't resist.

Socks in tow, they join the race,
Running fast, a silly chase.
Step by step, they trip and twirl,
Laughing loud in this mad whirl.

Who knew thoughts could take such flight,
Strapping up for silly plight?
They knot the tales of joy and cheer,
Endless giggles, come on near.

With every loop, a wish takes form,
In the craziest of norm.
These laces hold the laughter tight,
A band of dreams, oh what a sight!

Dreams Intertwined in Color

Colors clash, they intertwine,
In a swirl that's quite divine.
Brushes dance like they're alive,
Splashes here, oops, let's revive!

With red and blue, the art is grand,
Every hue takes its stand.
Green giggles and yellow grins,
Throw in purple, where fun begins!

Swirls of laughter in the air,
Tickled feet without a care.
Each stroke brings a spark of glee,
A canvas painted wild and free.

As daylight fades, the colors gleam,
A wacky, whirling dream team.
In this palette of joys galore,
Let's splash together and explore!

Bands of Unity and Vision

Join the crew, we're side by side,
Hand in hand, with hearts like tide.
Each one sportin' quirks and charms,
Together melting all alarm.

These bands we wear, a silly show,
Vibrant colors, watch them glow!
In sync we move, a silly dance,
Laughing loud, let's take the chance.

Every step, a joyful sound,
With every twist, we're joy unbound.
We leap as one, a crazy bunch,
Like a peanut butter and jelly crunch!

So join our team, don't be shy,
With every giggle, we will fly.
In this fun-filled, wacky spree,
We find our strength in harmony!

Bracelets of Shifting Realities

Wrap me up in memories bright,
A wiggly tale, a wondrous sight.
Bangles chatting, tales they spin,
In this realm, let the fun begin!

One minute wise, the next a clown,
Twisting truths, upside down.
A pop of color, then a wink,
My bracelets giggle, what will they think?

Misdirection is our game,
Changing lanes, never the same.
With every shake, realities bend,
In laughter's embrace, we transcend.

So stack them up, your wrist adored,
Let the quirky truths be explored.
In this world of whimsy wide,
Together we'll take that silly ride!

Visions Captured in Silken Ties

In a world where colors clash,
We wear our hopes as we dash.
Flares of fabric, bright and bold,
Stories of laughter waiting to be told.

Twisted loops on every wrist,
Create a future, you get the gist.
With every blink, a new surprise,
Fashioned fun beneath the skies.

Bouncing kids and grannies too,
Adorned in stripes of pink and blue.
Maybe it's silly, but we don't care,
Our tied-up dreams float in the air.

Zap! A spark, oh what a sight,
These silly ties feel just right.
Every giggle dances free,
In fabric friends, we find our glee!

Arteries of Anticipated Change

Twirling threads of laughter, we weave,
The kind of style that makes you believe.
Giggly knots, they make us grin,
Simple ties bring the fun within.

Each hue a promise of a joke,
Mismatched socks and silly smoke.
They giggle too, the ties are wise,
Tickling fancies 'neath the skies.

A twist here, a twirl there,
Frayed edges dancing without a care.
With every pull, the future sings,
In tie-dyed dreams of playful things!

An arm raised high with joy so pure,
These gentle straps, they will endure.
Wherever we go, we're part of the jest,
Our funny ties, we love the best!

Futures Adorned in Simple Straps

Slap on a color, let's take a ride,
Underneath our playful pride.
Every twist has a story to tell,
Laughter dances, oh so well.

Elastic dreams and kooky schemes,
Threaded laughter, sewn with seams.
Every strap, a spark of cheer,
Bringing bonkers memories near.

Here's a strap that plays a tune,
As we prance beneath the moon.
Who knew simple ties could play,
Such funny games all night and day?

So grab a loop and wear it tight,
Join the laughter, feel the light.
In every color, every hue,
Tomorrow laughs with me and you!

The Essence of Next Generation Threads

Threads of tomorrow, winks and grins,
Dancing on wrists, where fun begins.
Funky colors and shapes galore,
Silly giggles, we just want more!

Light as air, but lively too,
These strands have magic, who knew?
A tickle here, a jangle there,
We wear our smiles; they float in the air.

Bouncing like jelly on a plate,
Time for laughs, don't be late!
Straps that tease, just for fun,
In this zany race, we've already won!

So grab your loop, and let's parade,
In a world of bright serenades.
With every wave, we spin, we sway,
Tomorrow's threads are here to play!

Narratives Bound by Future's Thread

In a world of colorful dreams,
Each loop tells tales as it beams.
A twist and a turn, oh what a show,
Adventures await in the glow.

Straps that giggle at fortune's call,
Each promising fun, to rise and fall.
A flick of the wrist, and they cheer,
Join the mischief, there's nothing to fear.

With patterns that dance in the night,
Bringing laughter, oh what a sight!
Embrace the moment, the zany flair,
Decked out in stories we gladly share.

So slap on a tale, let it fly,
Hold onto joy as time passes by.
In threads of the future, we'll play our part,
Together we weave, oh joyous art!

Adornments of a Bright Destiny

Bangles of dreams with quirky charms,
Promising giggles and endless balms.
Each sparkly clasp just wants to dance,
Join in the madness, give life a chance.

Jelly-colored bands of gleeful hope,
Each stretchy moment, a perfect scope.
Wobbling with joy as they gently sway,
Our future is bright, come laugh and play.

With laughter stitched in every seam,
Adorn our wrists, let's create a dream.
Each snap of the wrist, a marvelous cheer,
A festivity blooms, with friends ever near.

So let's raise a toast, make it grand,
To trinkets of fun draped on each hand.
Dance with the rhythm of fate's own ring,
In these adornments, together we sing!

Eloquent Ties of Tomorrow

Colorful threads that giggle and tease,
All dressed up in whimsical ease.
A flick and a twist, laughter will swell,
In each little knot, there's a story to tell.

Twisted together, we laugh with glee,
Memories made, as bright as can be.
Snapping and clapping, each gesture a joke,
Our bonds of the future, a joyous yoke.

Patterns and shapes that dance and prance,
Who knew that tomorrow could look like this chance?
With every small tug, we pull it in tight,
Hitching our dreams in the softest light.

So gather your pals, those colorful ties,
With laughter and fun, we'll reach for the skies.
Bound by the future, in colors so bold,
In these eloquent ties, let the stories unfold!

Jewelry of Life's Next Chapter

Trinkets that spark with laughter and glee,
Adventures await for you and for me.
Each twist of the wrist sends a ripple of cheer,
Crafting our future, the horizon is near.

Slap it on quick, oh don't be shy,
These marvelous bands make time fly by.
With every new color and dainty add-on,
We craft a mosaic of stories, come on!

Rubber and metal all jumbled in style,
The blinks make us giggle, every once in a while.
A dance on the table can start with a snap,
In this jewelry realm, let's close the gap.

So flip through the future and tie up your fate,
Decking our wrists, we can't hesitate!
Our chapters unfold with each silly jest,
In life's next story, we dare to invest!

Future's Emblematic Embrace

With colors flashing, what a sight,
I wear my badge, oh what a delight!
Each slip of rubber, a silly grin,
Who knew the future would start with a spin?

I clasp my wrist, a link so neat,
A chorus of laughter fills the street.
Fashion's rebels, in playful protest,
We sport these bands, who's the best dressed?

They glow in the night, like stars that cheer,
An armory of jest, wipe away fear.
Stuffed with balloons, and chocolates galore,
My wrist is now ready for a candy store!

So here's our pledge, wrapped up in fun,
Band to band, we all are one.
Laughing together, in our own silly way,
Who knew a bracelet could save the day?

Stitches of Tomorrow's Tapestry

Look at my wrist, it's quite the tale,
A patchwork of colors that never go pale.
These funky loops, oh what a flair,
My friends wear them too, for we all care!

Each little band, a memory hugged tight,
With jokes in the mix, we dance through the night.
Every tug and pull, a giggle ensues,
Fashion forward, with whimsical hues!

In this future stitched, with laughter we sway,
The world is our canvas, let playtime stay.
So much to share, in swirling delight,
These quirky threads make all moments bright.

Come join the crew, of the stitched and the banded,
With whimsy and joy, our fun is always candid.
Together we weave, with stories to share,
In this tapestry of laughter, we float through the air!

Interlaced with Tomorrow's Light

Tangled together, what a strange sight,
Our bands catch the sun, making day bright.
Colors that clash, like an artist's spree,
Wrist rave in motion, come dance with me!

A twist and a twirl, parade of delight,
Each bounce in my step sends joy in full flight.
Gather 'round quickly, don't miss the fun,
As we weave tales in the light of the sun!

These elastics of joy, a playful embrace,
Bouncing through life, with smiles on our face.
Snap, crackle, pop, it's a friendship song,
With laughter and fun, we can do no wrong!

Let's fashion a future, so full of cheer,
With these cheerful bands that bring us all near.
Energized by curiosity's plight,
We'll dance to the rhythm of interlaced light!

The Path Seamed in Colors Bright

On this journey we go, with bands loud and proud,
Together we stomp, dance, and laugh out loud.
A rainbow of smiles, as we skip down the track,
Wait till we reach, and unleash the snack!

We're weaving a tale of joy and delight,
With quirky designs, oh, what a sight!
Arms interlocked, as we prance through the park,
These colorful threads ignite all our sparks!

Through puddles we splash, amid giggles and glee,
The world is our canvas, wild and free.
With each silly twist of colorful flair,
The path appears brighter when friends are all there!

So skip with abandon, let laughter ignite,
Our journey is stitched with joy, oh so bright.
As we dance down the lane, let our spirits take flight,
For the path we have sewn will always feel right!

www.ingramcontent.com/pod-product-compliance
Lightning Source LLC
Chambersburg PA
CBHW070306120526
44590CB00017B/2575